Birds up close

How Birds Fly

A Bobbie Kalman Book

🌱 Crabtree Publishing Company

Birds up close
A Bobbie Kalman Book

**For Cyril and Joy,
who share their love of birds**

Editor-in-Chief
Bobbie Kalman

Writing team
Bobbie Kalman
Jacqueline Langille
Niki Walker

Managing editor
Lynda Hale

Series editor
Niki Walker

Editors
Greg Nickles
Virginia Mainprize

Text and photo research
Jacqueline Langille

Computer design
Lynda Hale
Andy Gecse (cover concept)

Consultant
Ron Rohrbaugh, Cornell Laboratory of Ornithology

Production coordinator
Hannelore Sotzek

Photographs
Russell C. Hansen: back cover, pages 11, 15, 16, 17, 18, 29
Robert J. Huffman/Field Mark Publications: pages 21, 28 (top)
Robert McCaw: pages 26-27
Dave Taylor: page 20
Valan Photos: John Mitchell: page 27 (top);
   Dennis W. Schmidt: page 30
Other photographs by Digital Vision

Illustrations
All illustrations by Doug Swinamer, except the following:
   Barbara Bedell: page 10 (top)

Printer
Worzalla Publishing Company

Color separations and film
Dot 'n Line Image Inc.

Crabtree Publishing Company

350 Fifth Avenue
Suite 3308
New York
N.Y. 10118

360 York Road, RR 4,
Niagara-on-the-Lake,
Ontario, Canada
L0S 1J0

73 Lime Walk
Headington
Oxford OX3 7AD
United Kingdom

Cataloging in Publication Data
Kalman, Bobbie
   How birds fly

(Birds up close)
Includes index.

ISBN 0-86505-754-0 (library bound)   ISBN 0-86505-768-0 (pbk.)
This book introduces the basic concepts of bird flight, including lift
and thrust, takeoff, landing, migration, and the anatomy of birds.

1. Birds—Flight—Juvenile literature. [1. Birds—Flight.] I. Title.
II. Series: Kalman, Bobbie. Birds up close.

QL698.7.K345 1997   j573.7′9818   LC 97-31453
                                                                              CIP

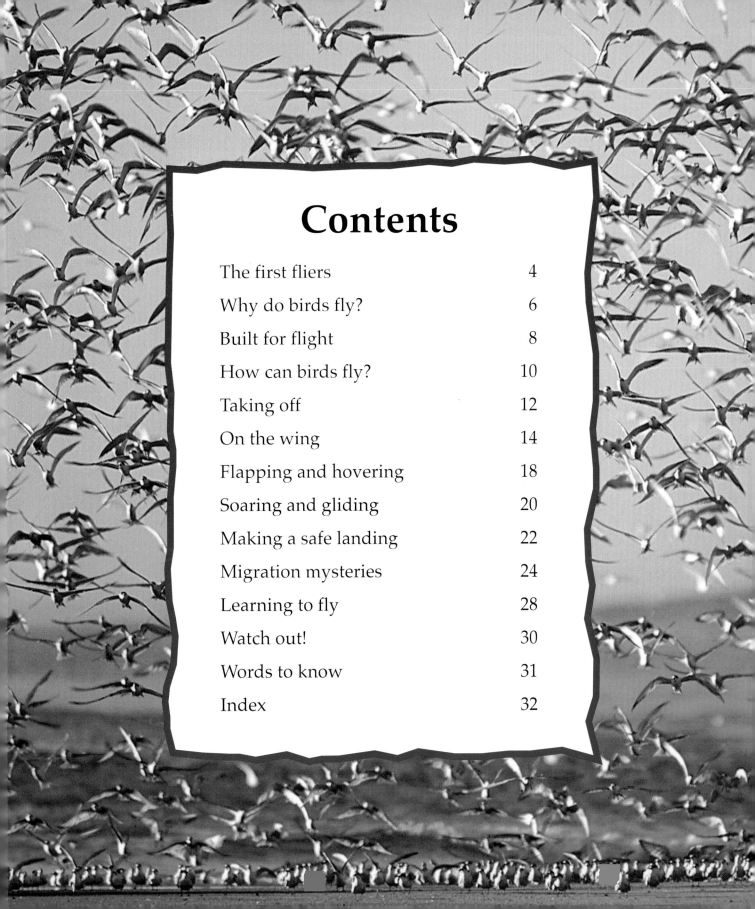

Contents

The first fliers

Birds have been on earth for over 100 million years. The first birds lived at the time of the dinosaurs. Scientists believe that reptiles were the ancestors of birds. Over millions of years, the reptiles slowly changed, or **evolved**, into birds.

Change to survive

Animals evolve in order to survive. As birds slowly evolved, they became better able to escape danger, find food, and defend themselves.

2. A flap of skin grew between their front and hind legs. The reptiles began to jump farther. They used the flaps of skin to glide from tree to tree.

1. Some scaly reptiles began climbing trees to escape from enemies. They leapt from branch to branch.

4. *The early birds began to flap their wings and fly. By flying, they could easily escape from enemies on the ground and in the trees.*

3. *Over millions of years, feathers replaced the reptiles' scales and covered the flaps of skin between the front and hind legs. Birds are the only animals with feathers.*

The Archaeopteryx
The first animal that looked like a bird was the archaeopteryx. Its name means "ancient wing." The archaeopteryx crawled in trees like a reptile. It probably did not fly but glided from tree to tree.

Why do birds fly?

Flying may look like fun, but birds do not fly to have a good time. They fly in order to survive. Flying helps birds stay alive by allowing them to spot food and escape from danger quickly.

Fly or fight?

Most birds have enemies, or **predators**, on the ground and in trees. Predators are animals that hunt and eat other animals for food. Predators that hunt birds include wild cats, weasels, rats, hawks and other birds of prey, and humans. Most birds do not defend themselves by fighting. When a bird notices that a predator is getting close, it quickly takes off and flies out of its enemy's reach.

A bird can spot food more easily from high in the sky than from the ground. It can also reach seeds and fruits in the tops of trees and bushes.

Protecting their home

Many birds build their nest in a tree or on a cliff high above the ground. From these high places, birds can see a predator long before it reaches their nest. If an animal comes too close, birds swoop and fly towards it to scare it away from the nest.

(above) Birds attack fast-moving prey from the air. Although fish are able to swim quickly, an eagle can easily grab one. The fish cannot see the eagle in the air, so it cannot avoid being caught.

Built for flight

Bird bodies are perfect for flight. They are lightweight, but they are powerful. The sleek, or **streamlined**, shape of birds helps them slip easily through the air. During flight, a bird tucks its legs against its body and becomes even more streamlined. Feathers help smooth the body from head to tail.

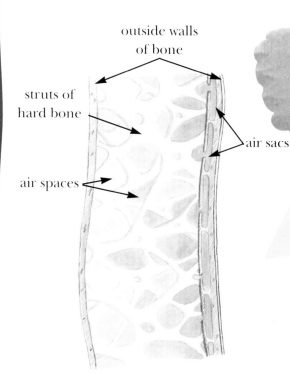

outside walls of bone

struts of hard bone

air sacs

air spaces

*Bird bones are hollow. They have **struts** and air sacs for added strength. A strut is a bar, brace, or other supporting piece inside the bone.*

Light bodies

"Light as a feather" is a good phrase to describe birds. Birds do not have teeth, so their head does not weigh much. The rest of their body also weighs very little because their bones are hollow. **Air sacs** in their bones help birds "float" through the air. Air sacs are small pouches filled with air.

Muscle power

Even with such light bodies, birds need a lot of power to fly. They have strong chest muscles, so they can flap their wings with great force. Hard-working muscles need energy. Energy comes from food, so birds need to keep eating. Some eat half their weight in food each day!

Airplanes and birds both have a streamlined shape. Some birds, such as the sea gull on the left, look similar to an airplane when they fly.

Feathers

A bird has three main types of feathers: **contour**, **flight**, and **down**. Contour feathers cover most of the bird's body and give it a sleek shape. Flight feathers, located on the tail and wings, help the bird get off the ground and steer. Small, fluffy down feathers lie next to the skin under the contour feathers. Down helps keep the bird warm.

Closeup of a feather

*Contour and flight feathers have tiny parts called **barbules** that lock together in the same way zippers do.*

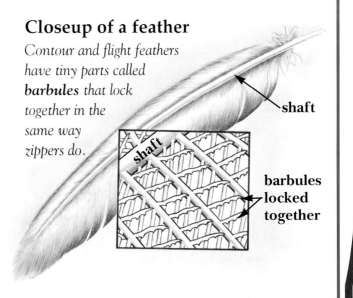

shaft

shaft

barbules locked together

How can birds fly?

For thousands of years, people dreamed of flying like birds. They built many different machines to get them off the ground. None of these machines worked well, however, because people did not understand the two forces that are needed for flying—**lift** and **thrust**.

People built flapping and gliding machines to try to fly like birds. These machines never flew as well as birds can.

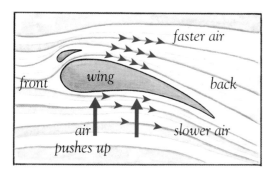

Some scientists call the way wings create lift Bernoulli's law. In science, a law describes something that always happens under certain conditions or because of certain actions.

Lifting up

Birds use the air and their wing shape to create lift. When a bird flaps its wings, air flows over and under them, moving from the front of the wings to the back. Air flowing over the wings must reach the back of the wings at the same time as the air flowing under them. The air on top has to travel farther, so it moves faster. The slower-moving air underneath pushes up on the wing and creates lift. By flapping its wings, the bird uses lift to rise into the air.

When the wings move down, the wing feathers move close together to push the air with great force.

Thrusting forward

Once a bird is off the ground, it has to keep moving through the air. Just as swimmers push themselves through water with their arms, birds push themselves through air with their wings. When a bird pushes against the air, the movement creates thrust.

←wind

When the wings move up, the wing feathers spread apart. Air slides easily between them.

Taking off

In some ways, a bird's takeoff is like that of an airplane. An airplane speeds down a runway so that air will move quickly over its wings to create lift. Just as airplanes drive quickly down runways before leaving the ground, some birds run to gain enough speed to lift off. Other birds do not need to run for takeoff. They flap their wings quickly to create lift.

No runway

Most airplanes take off from a runway, but many birds do not need one. Web-footed birds push against the water during takeoff. Others leap into the air from cliffs or trees.

Stormy weather

In many ways, a bird's takeoff is different than that of an airplane. An airplane must keep its wings level during takeoff so it does not flip over. Airplanes avoid flying during wind storms because their stiff metal wings cannot change shape enough to stay level. On the other hand, a strong wind usually makes it easier for birds to take off. They often try to take off into the wind because wind increases the lift under their wings.

On the wing

Birds use their wings to move through the air. While flying, they flap their wings or hold them out straight and glide. Each wing is made up of many parts. The bones in a bird's wing have the same names as those in a person's arm. The wing has a shoulder, elbow, wrist, and finger bones at the tip.

*Underneath the feathers, skin, and muscles, a bird's wing is made up of bones and **tendons**. Tendons are like cords that connect muscles to bones.*

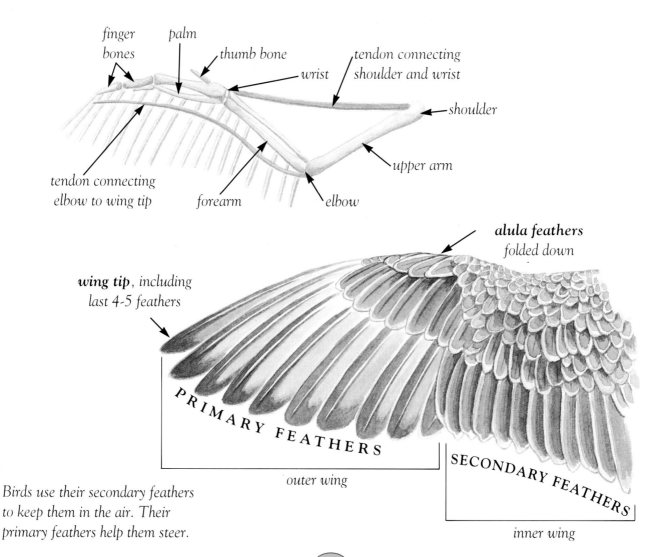

finger bones

palm

thumb bone

wrist

tendon connecting shoulder and wrist

shoulder

tendon connecting elbow to wing tip

forearm

elbow

upper arm

alula feathers folded down

wing tip, *including last 4-5 feathers*

PRIMARY FEATHERS

outer wing

SECONDARY FEATHERS

inner wing

Birds use their secondary feathers to keep them in the air. Their primary feathers help them steer.

To flap, birds stretch their wings upward and push them down through the air.

The inner wing

Two parts of the wing work together for flying—the inner wing and the outer wing. The inner wing is the part between a bird's elbow and wrist. It is used mainly for lift. The **secondary feathers** along its edge form a smooth surface over which air flows, helping the bird stay in the air.

The outer wing

The outer wing is the part between the wrist and the wing tip. Birds move the outer wing with their wrist. The **flight** or **primary feathers** along the outer wing are used for thrust. They also help the bird steer.

Slowing down

To slow down, a bird tilts its wings, causing the air to curl, or flow less smoothly, over each wing. When the air curls, less lift pushes up on the wings. The bird slows down because of the reduced lift. A bird can **stall** and fall through the air if it loses too much lift, however.

Preventing a stall

To prevent a stall, the bird raises a special part of each wing called an **alula**. An alula is a small group of feathers attached to a bird's thumb. The feathers lift up to help the air pass a little more smoothly over the wing. Without alulas, birds would stall and crash.

alula

wind

wind

alula

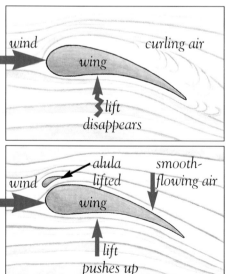

wind wing *curling air*
lift disappears

When a bird tilts its wing to slow down, air curls around the wing. The curling air does not provide lift and causes the bird to stall.

alula lifted *smooth-flowing air*
wind wing
lift pushes up

The raised alula prevents stalling. It makes the air flow more smoothly over the tilted wing so that lift is not lost and the bird does not crash.

Changing direction

To steer in a different direction, birds change the position of their wings. This bird is making a right turn. It lowers its right wing and lifts its left one. It then flaps its left wing harder, which moves the wing forward. The right wing falls back, causing the bird's body to swing to the right.

Turning tail

The bird also uses its tail to turn. This bird has spread its tail feathers to begin turning. The tail is twisted higher on one side. Wind pushes on the high side of the tail and swings the bird around. Birds with large tails can turn sharply at high speeds. Birds with smaller tails cannot steer as well.

Making a right turn

The left wing is raised and moves forward.

The tail feathers are spread and part of the tail is twisted up.

The right wing is lowered.

The bird swings to its right.

Flapping and hovering

The most common type of flight is called **flapping flight**. For flapping flight, a bird flaps its wings nonstop. It is the most tiring way to fly. Birds use a lot of energy when they flap their wings for a long time.

Bounding flight

To save energy, small birds use **bounding flight**. When bounding, birds do not flap their wings nonstop. They dip down toward the ground and flap their wings quickly to gain speed. When they are flying fast enough, they fold their wings and swing their body upward. The speed they gained on the way down allows them to sail up through the air. On their way down, they start flapping again.

This diagram shows how a bounding bird flaps its wings to gain speed and then swings up to gain height. Birds bound only for a short time.

This bounding cardinal is on the upswing. Its wings are folded so that its body is more streamlined.

18

Hovering

Some small birds can **hover**, or hang in one place in the air. Hovering is the most difficult type of flying. The bird's wings flap very quickly, but the bird stays in one place. Hummingbirds are the most famous hovering birds.

They can hover for several minutes in front of a flower to drink nectar. They do not move from their spot. Another bird that hovers well is the hoopoe, shown in the picture above. Hoopoes hover at their nests to feed their babies.

Soaring and gliding

Large birds have two ways to save energy when they fly. They can use air currents to travel and not need to flap their wings at all. This type of flight is called **soaring**. **Gliding** is also an easy way to fly—a bird just holds out its wings and lets the wind carry it along.

Soaring

Warm air rises, and cool air falls. When the air over land is heated by the sun, it rises in columns called **thermals**. A bird can soar on these thermals. It spreads its wings and is lifted by the rising air. When the bird gets high enough, it simply moves out of the thermal and glides until it finds another one.

When they search for food, vultures soar on thermals for many hours every day.

Many seabirds use both soaring and gliding to fly over the ocean. They soar on the strong winds that blow up off the high waves. They glide on the air over calmer waters and then soar up on the strong winds that blow off the next waves. Some seabirds such as albatrosses can stay in the air for up to eight hours a day.

Gliding flight

Gliding is another relaxed way of flying.
Birds simply stretch out their wings and float
on the wind. They do not have to flap or use
any muscle power to glide. They can glide
for long distances on a strong wind.

Undulating flight

Larger birds use a combination of flapping
and gliding to save energy. They glide slowly
toward the ground, flap to gain height, and
then glide down again. This up-and-down
flying is called **undulating** flight.

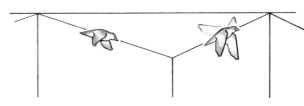

*In undulating flight, the bird saves
energy by gliding.*

*Wind and lift keep
the bird up in the air.*

*Air pushes up on
the bird's wings,
causing lift.*

*Gravity pulls the
bird slowly down
toward the ground.*

*When gliding, birds carefully balance the force of lift with the
force of gravity. Gravity slowly pulls them down, but a strong
wind gives birds lift and helps them stay in the air.*

Making a safe landing

Landing is the most difficult part of flying. Birds need **judgment** and skill to make safe landings. Judgment is a bird's ability to figure out the distance to its landing area, as well as knowing how hard the wind is blowing. Birds need skill to slow down and land at just the right moment. Hitting the ground too hard could injure a bird's feet and legs.

In the air, birds use their "brakes" to slow down for a perfect landing. Most birds swing their body into an up-and-down position so that they are no longer streamlined. They tilt their wings against the wind and spread their tail feathers. The alula feathers raise to help air pass smoothly over the wings. Finally, their legs absorb the force of hitting the ground or a branch.

Crash landing

Some birds find it very difficult to land. A few types of birds can land only on the water. They glide down quickly and slide along the water until they coast to a stop. Seabirds with large wings need a brisk wind to land on the ground. They often stall when they slow down, and the wind helps them coast to the ground. If there is no wind, they crash-land. Their feet absorb the first force of hitting the ground. They then fall forward onto their well-padded chest.

Migration mysteries

Each spring, flocks of birds fly north to their breeding grounds, where they nest and raise their young. At the end of August, these birds **migrate**, or travel, south where they stay until the next breeding season. Migration is the round trip that birds make each year from southern areas to their breeding grounds.

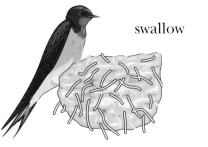

jay

oriole

swallow

robin

Reproducing, *or making babies, is the most important part of a bird's life. To raise their young, many birds migrate to find safe places with plenty of food. They also need more daylight hours to find enough food for their babies.*

In search of the sun

Why do birds leave warm southern places to head north again each spring? Since most birds are active only in the daytime, scientists believe they move to places with more daylight. In summer, the days are longer in the north. The birds have more time to gather food for their chicks than they would in the south.

When do birds migrate?

Many birds leave their northern homes long before food runs out or the weather becomes cooler. Some scientists believe that shorter days may be a signal for birds to head south.

Migration routes

Birds have followed the same **migration routes** for thousands of years. Some birds fly across oceans from northern places to their southern homes. Other birds fly across land from the east to the west.

Built-in compasses

Scientists know that birds migrating in the daytime use the sun as a guide, and birds that travel at night use the stars to show them the way. Scientists still are not sure, however, about how birds navigate when the skies are cloudy. They think birds may have a built-in compass that tells them where to fly.

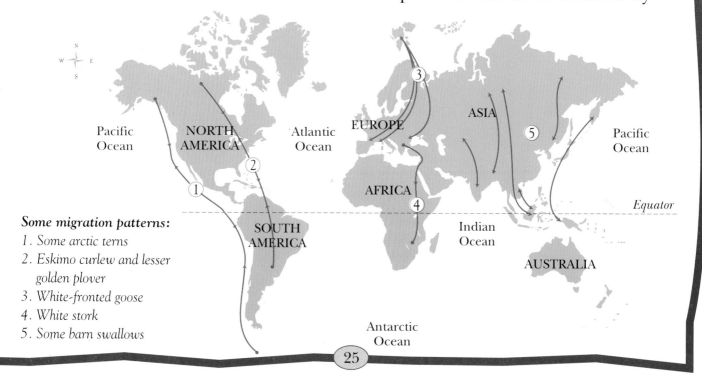

Pacific Ocean

NORTH AMERICA

Atlantic Ocean

EUROPE

ASIA

Pacific Ocean

AFRICA

SOUTH AMERICA

Indian Ocean

Equator

AUSTRALIA

Antarctic Ocean

Some migration patterns:
1. *Some arctic terns*
2. *Eskimo curlew and lesser golden plover*
3. *White-fronted goose*
4. *White stork*
5. *Some barn swallows*

Flying in a V

Have you ever looked up and seen a large V moving across the sky? This V is a flock of migrating geese or ducks. Flying in a V pattern helps birds save energy during their long trip. Each bird gets some lift from the bird ahead. This extra lift makes it easier to fly because the birds do not have to flap as much to stay in the air. The leader gets no free lift, however, so different birds take turns leading the flock.

Some arctic terns migrate the distance of four trips across the United States.

And the winner is...

Twice a year, the Arctic tern sets the record for the longest bird migration. In summer, Arctic terns nest in the northern parts of Asia, Europe, and Canada. Before winter, they migrate to places in the southern Pacific, Atlantic, and Antarctic oceans. They like to live in places with the most daylight hours. Some Arctic terns travel up to 11,000 miles (17 700 km) each way!

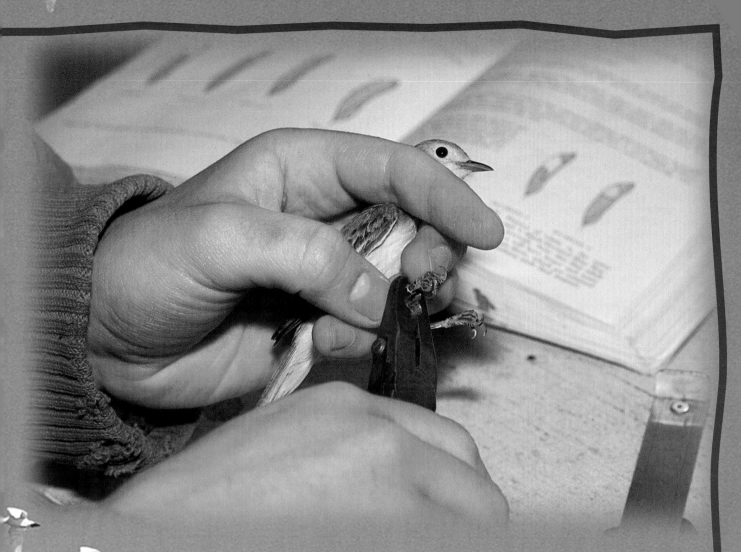

Bird banding

Scientists around the world use a banding program to find out more about birds. People catch birds in a net or trap that does not hurt them. They then put a loose metal band with a number and a return address around each bird's leg. People who find a banded bird after it has been released contact the scientists at the return address. They send the scientists information about when and where the bird was recaptured.

Banding programs allow scientists to know where birds migrate, how far they travel, and how fast they fly. For example, a bird banded in Cape Cod, Massachusetts, was found six days later on the Caribbean island of Martinique, which is 1,900 miles (3000 km) away!

Learning to fly

Baby birds are called **chicks** or **nestlings**. Some have no feathers when they are born. They stay in the nest until they can fly. Other baby birds are born covered with down. Soon after downy chicks hatch, they follow their parents out of the nest.

Soon after downy chicks are born, they follow their parents out of the nest to look for food. This baby Canada goose found a juicy dandelion to eat.

Nestlings such as the bokmakieries in the picture below do not leave the nest for up to three weeks after they hatch.

Growing feathers and muscles

Baby birds grow quickly. Their chest muscles grow stronger every day. The chicks often stand up in the nest to stretch and practice flapping their wings. They must wait for all their contour and flight feathers to grow in before they can fly.

The flying instinct

All flying birds know how to take to the air as soon as they grow flight feathers. Knowing how to do something, such as flying, without being taught is called **instinct**.

Leaving the nest

When a young bird's body is ready for flight, the bird leaves its nest. If the nest is on the ground or in a fallen log, the bird simply takes off. If the nest is built high above the ground, the babies must leave it the hard way! As they get bigger, there is less room in the nest and they get squeezed out. Instinct tells them to flap their wings before they hit the ground.

Young birds can fly when their flight feathers have grown. This bluebird is on its first flight out of the nest box.

Swallows are great fliers, but young ones need their parents to teach them how to catch flying insects for food. Some people have seen swallows pass food to their young in midair!

Watch out

Flying may save birds from danger on the ground, but there is still plenty of danger in the air. While flying, birds must be careful to avoid crashing into many things, including buildings, fences, cars, and electric wires.

Broken wings

When birds are flying quickly or looking for food, they may not see power lines or wire fences. If their wing hits a wire, their bones break. Birds with broken wings often die.

Window pains

Once in a while, a bird crashes into a window. A bird's hollow bones break easily, and a wing often gets broken. An injured bird usually falls to the ground and dies.

Roads kill

From the air at night, a wet road looks like a river. If water birds land on a road, they cannot take off. Before they can move out of the way, a car or truck may run over them. Flying low across a highway is also dangerous for birds. They can be hit by speeding cars.

The sharp spikes on barbed-wire fences are dangerous. If a bird flies into barbed wire, it often gets caught and starves to death.

Words to know

air current Air constantly flowing in a certain stream or along the same path

alula A small group of feathers attached to a bird's thumb

barbules Tiny parts of a feather that lock together

bounding flight A type of energy-saving flight used by small birds

chick A baby bird

contour feathers Long, smooth feathers that cover most of a bird's body

down feathers The soft feathers between a bird's skin and its contour feathers

evolve To change slowly in order to survive

flapping flight A type of flight during which birds flap their wings nonstop

flight feathers Long feathers on the edges of the wings and tail that help a bird fly

gliding The act of holding wings out straight and floating on the wind

hovering The act of flapping wings quickly and staying in one place

instinct Knowledge of how to do something without being taught

judgment The ability to figure out things such as distance and speed

lift A force needed in flight; lift is caused by air moving over a wing

migrate To move from one place to another in order to find food or a safe place to raise young

nestling A baby bird

predator An animal that hunts and eats other animals for food

primary and secondary feathers The two types of flight feathers on wings

soaring The act of a bird rising upward on warm air currents

stall To stop air from moving over wings, causing a bird to fall

streamlined Describing something with a smooth, sleek shape

thermal A column of warm air that rises over land

thrust A force needed in flight to move forward through the air

undulating flight An energy-saving flight that uses gliding and flapping

Index

1 2 3 4 5 6 7 8 9 0   Printed in the U.S.A.   6 5 4 3 2 1 0 9 8 7